Dear Jack,

This is a book about beauty in desolate places, about flowers blooming in harsh landscapes. Kinda the story of your life! What strength it must take, what energy and will. In the end, those are the things which are undefeatable.

Love,
Dick, Laurie, Jane, Chris, Jenny & Duke.

DESERTLANDS
of
AMERICA

J.A. KRAULIS

DESERTLANDS
of
AMERICA

GALLERY BOOKS
An Imprint of W. H. Smith Publishers Inc.
112 Madison Avenue
New York City 10016

Produced by Discovery Books for:
Gallery Books
An imprint of W.H. Smith Publishers Inc.
112 Madison Avenue
New York, New York 10016

ISBN: 0-8317-2195-2

Design: Michael van Elsen
Typesetting: Robinson Communications Group
Printed and bound in Italy

88 89 90 91 6 5 4 3 2 1

ACKNOWLEDGMENTS

Several people helped me significantly in the creation of *Desertlands*, including Johny van Nieuwkerk, Baiba and Pat Morrow, Wendy and Jeremy Schmidt, and Catherine Young and Bo Curtis. Pat and Jeremy introduced me to many stunningly beautiful, hidden places in the desert which I otherwise might never have seen. Cathy and Bo provided invaluable navigational assistance by land, in the air and over water. Because of his skills as a pilot and his matchless understanding of the requirements of aerial photography, Bo shares at least half the credit for each of the photos on pages 8, 18, 62, 63, 78-79, 81, 85, 90, 100, 101, 105 and 110.

My wife, Linda Küttis, accompanied me on most of my trips into the desert, encouraged the rest, helped immeasurably in refining the picture selection, and took the photographs on pages 77, 98, 115 and 122.

Page 2: Through a break in the clouds, sunlight illuminates fins of sandstone as dark thunderstorms move into Ernie's Country, a seldom-visited part of Canyonlands National Park, Utah.

CONTENTS

A seep-moistened wall at the bottom of Orderville Canyon, Utah, reflects the golden glow from the sunlit upper reaches.

For Linda
and
For Little Anna

INTRODUCTION

The deserts of America contain many places that are spectacular, and many that are strange. Silvery, shimmering salt flats have sterilized large areas, and purple-black volcanic cones have devastated others. Above and below tablelands rise and drop cliffs the color of pearl or gold or fire. Grooved badlands, sometimes rounded, sometimes sharply ridged, come in browns, blues and grays, while some are burgundy and others mustard.

For every nuance of color in the earth and the rock, there is an unusual, even improbable shape. There are buttes, towers and hoodoos; grottos, canyons and chasms; dunes, cinder cones and lava flows; arches and natural bridges. The deserts of the American southwest contain a bewildering collection of surfaces and shapes, colors and materials, a petrified catalogue of landscapes that defies all generalizations.

Not all of this region is a parade of geological marvels. A passing motorist might find most of it empty and lonely, even boring. Much of the terrain is nearly flat, and most seems to hold nothing more than stones and bushes, an unremitting, dull gray-green land under a blank sky, where the sun and the temperature go up and down but nothing much else happens. The casual visitor may never see anything so interesting as a dune field or a cactus forest.

But there is plenty of gold amidst the gravel. One of the paradoxes of the American deserts is that, while relentless in apparent sameness over considerable distances, they also contain many remarkable and indeed unique places. It would take more than a lifetime to explore them all. For a start, there are eleven national parks and more than two dozen national monuments. They are noteworthy not only for their number, but for their dissimilarities. While other regions, such as the Canadian Rockies, contain many national parks, these tend to share a common character. However, not a single one of the national parks in the American southwest resembles any of the others in its prominent features.

Left: The fantastic towers and buttes of Monument Valley, Arizona, are all that remains of a once-continuous mesa that was cracked by uplifting and has been mostly carried away by erosion.

Then there are the national recreation areas, the state parks and recreation areas, Indian tribal parks, and federal- and state-designated wilderness and primitive areas. Many extraordinary places, on the other hand, have no protected status at all, and some don't even have names.

In the American southwest, there are four major deserts. The Sonoran Desert occupies most of southern Arizona and the adjacent part of California, continuing far into Mexico along both sides of the Gulf of California. Northwards, the arid land becomes the Mojave Desert, which includes most of the eastern half of southern California and the southern tip of Nevada. The Great Basin Desert spans almost all the rest of Nevada and most of Utah, as well as bordering portions of California, Oregon, Idaho, Wyoming, Colorado, New Mexico and Arizona. Most of the Chihuahuan Desert lies in Mexico, but it extends into large areas of Texas and New Mexico.

Desertlands of America contains photographs from each of these four deserts, but rather than attempt to differentiate among these biologically classified regions, it treats the deserts, basically most of the American southwest, as a whole. The book is primarily about landscapes, about special places. It attempts to show the beautiful and the exceptional rather than the typical.

A large portion of the photos come from the Colorado Plateau, so called because it is drained by the Colorado River. The centerpiece of the American deserts, this part of the Great Basin Desert has the lion's share of dramatic landscapes, claiming eight out of the eleven national parks (including Grand Canyon), as well as the splendid Painted Desert.

Some of the photos come from places on the periphery of the desert, perhaps not quite *in* the desert by the strictest criteria, but definitely related to it. The intention was to select photos that would celebrate the rich diversity of the land, rather than to be overly fussy about botanical boundaries, which differ according to which authority one accepts.

There are places such as Bryce Canyon, which, according to the maps, lies within the general boundaries of the desert, but which has stately stands of ponderosa pine and is obviously not desert. Yet it demands inclusion in a primarily landscape book on the desert. The very strangeness of its geological formations, the stands of exposed red rock, seem to belong only in the desert. It is also the uppermost and most recently deposited step in a great geological staircase, the lower tiers of which consist of Zion and the Grand Canyon.

Where desert ends and grassland or forest begins can shift with changes in climate and can be a marked or a very gradual transition. Most of the Grand Canyon, for example, falls outside the Painted Desert, according to small-scale maps, and impressive forests are found on both rims. But desert vegetation begins abruptly over the edge, and Phantom Ranch, at the bottom of the Canyon, has an annual average temperature 25° F higher than that of the North Rim six miles away, which in turn gets nearly three times as much rain and more than six hundred times as much snow.

The deserts are fascinating in their extremes, their contradictions. In the driest of climates are found the most fluid of landscapes, where the wind ripples waves of graceful sand dunes. Places oppressively hot by day freeze at night. Country lacking water can be scoured by the most violent of floods. Sparse, dull growth erupts in blooms as extravagant and colorful as those of any environment. In an open land, great canyons remain invisible until the visitor is but a few paces away from their edge.

Perhaps the biggest paradox of the desert, particularly of the Colorado Plateau, is this: lacking the peace and shade of forests, leagues removed from the restless drama of the sea, devoid of shimmering glaciers reaching heavenward, and containing no natural freshwater lakes or crystal clear rivers, this region is still one of the most supremely beautiful in the world. There are many who would concede it is the ultimate landscape, sometimes intimidating and often utterly magnificent.

FROM SAND TO SANDSTONE

Sunlit, the barrens are bright enough to cause snow blindness. Clean, white drifts sweep across the land towards stark, distant mountains. The road into the area has been recently cleared, and only the banks thrown up by the plow guide the way through the vacant, wind-scoured terrain. A more wintry-looking place would be hard to find. But this is not the Arctic, and the drifts are not snow.

One needs to walk barefoot to break the illusion, and to revel fully in the uncommon purity of White Sands National Monument, New Mexico. This clean, undulating sea of gypsum, its wind-driven waves imperceptibly surging forward in geological time, is absolutely white, completely free of any hue or tone. Sensuous and serene, it is a magic place, especially after sunset when the dunes are imbued with the blue of dusk and the sky is rimmed with pink.

However, White Sands is an anomaly, not only because of its extraordinary whiteness, but because dunes are the exception rather than the rule in the deserts of the United States. To be sure, there are other pockets of sand in the southwest. Light tan dunes are found in Death Valley and near Yuma, Arizona, dark gray volcanic dunes on the east side of Mono Lake in California and orange-pink dunes in several places on the Colorado Plateau. Ironically, the biggest dunes in America lie beyond the biologically designated boundaries of the major deserts. Great Sand Dunes National Monument in southeastern Colorado has small mountains of sand that crest seven hundred feet above their surroundings.

Great Sand Dunes is almost always a windy place where it is more comfortable to stand than to sit in order to avoid the stinging grains bouncing by the billions a couple of feet off the dune surfaces.

Left: The tracks of two beetles cross a sand dune in Death Valley National Monument, California.

Places where it is worth removing one's shoes are relatively rare in the southwest, however. Much more prevalent than fluid fields of sand dunes are other kinds of desert surfaces. In a land where most runoff never reaches the sea, but collects and evaporates, many expansive salt flats grow, those of southeastern California and around Great Salt Lake in Utah being among the best known. Alluvial fans, great skirts of gravel and stones, spread out from all the abundant mountain ranges, and recent volcanic outpourings are evident throughout the region.

In extreme contrast, not far north of the soft smooth White Sands lie black, menacingly ragged lava beds. Much farther north, Craters of the Moon National Monument in Idaho is one of the best examples of such an extruded, recently molten land. It is a place where one steps carefully, where a stumble onto the porous, tortuously jagged ground would result in scores of painful cuts and bruises. But not all the fire-born landscapes are threatening to the walker. Loose, tinkling cinders cover some volcanic cones, such as Sunset Crater, just beyond the edge of the desert near Flagstaff, Arizona. So delicate are the slopes that even foot travel is prohibited on this crater, which erupted less than a thousand years ago.

Among the materials of the desert are some uncommon ones. East of Holbrook, Arizona, rapidly eroding badlands reveal fields of crystal logs. Fossilized trunks lie around in abundance in Petrified Forest National Park, and although there isn't a chip of wood left amongst them, their resemblance to the originals is amazing. One can distinguish concentric rings, the "bark" layer and individual "knots," as well as the stumps of "roots." The quartz that has replaced the original wood has a beauty all its own, stained with impurities to form rainbows of glossy color.

Petrified Forest is a window on a far distant past, when dinosaurs slogged through swamps and trees as stately as Douglas firs grew there. At other times, shallow seas covered the area, and some of the rocks we see in the desert now were deposited then. But most noteworthy is the fact that the land that is desert today was once desert before. For of all the materials of which the desert is made, none is as significant to the unique landscape of the southwest as the bare stone known as slickrock.

Slickrock is, for the most part, sandstone: Wingate, Navajo and Entrada sandstone as well as much older de Chelly sandstone. Sandstone is to Nature what marble was to Michelangelo. It is a most versatile material, which the forces of erosion have cleaved, chipped and ground into fantastic forms.

A very large portion of the marvels of the Colorado Plateau are fashioned out of the sandstones, the most dominant being the Navajo, 2,000 feet thick in places. The great precipices of Zion, the domed cliffs of

Capitol Reef, the pinnacles and mazes of Canyonlands, the arches of Arches, the towers of Monument Valley, the tributary canyons of Glen Canyon and many more are all sandstone.

Some surfaces of the sandstone are honeycombed, a network of countless miniature grottos. Some are rough hewn and boldly shaped, others are rounded and polished, while still others are fine grained and delicately striated. Many are beautifully striped and streaked, with the cross-bedding of the original sand layers, the whitewash of alkali and the black gloss of manganese oxide, known as desert varnish. The last two are deposited by films of water trickling down the rock. Such variously etched and painted sandstone walls exist in uncountable numbers, and each can be appreciated as some grand, exquisite mural, a rich work of abstract art.

Most of this sandstone is made from the sand of ancient dunes. As has been mentioned, sand dunes in the southwest today are relatively rare and isolated. But it was not always so. At a time when the continents of North America and Europe were joined, drifting in some other sector of the planet, the land was a prehistoric Arabia, a vast ocean of shifting sand. As the eons passed, the sand was buried under other deposits, covered by the sea and turned to stone.

Resurrected to stretch again across horizons, in the strong light and in the clear air, these petrified sands perhaps explain as well as anything why the Colorado Plateau contains landscapes so splendid and so profound. This is the true desert primeval; the desert of today was born of the sands of deserts of long ago.

*The dune fields of White Sands, New Mexico,
become especially peaceful and sensuous at dusk.*

*A wind-rippled dune of pure gypsum in White Sands
National Monument, Tularosa Basin, New Mexico.*

Left: An aerial view of a pocket of sand dunes in a roadless region south of Monument Valley, Arizona.

Above: The first light of day leaves long shadows and brings out beguiling forms in the sand dunes of Death Valley National Monument.

The fantasyland of formations in Bryce Canyon
National Park, Utah, has been eroded from soft
sedimentary rocks that were originally deposited in a
lake bed.

North of Cameron, Arizona. Small hills of bentonite,
the rain-washed deposits of volcanic ash, are part of
the extraordinarily varied and colorful surface of the
Painted Desert.

Strong winds that often alternate in direction have
created the largest dunes in America at Great Sand
Dunes National Monument, Colorado, a piece of
Arabia beyond the boundaries of the major
southwest deserts.

22

The dunes near Stovepipe Wells are part of the extraordinary wealth of desert landforms found in Death Valley, California.

Above: Uncovered by the erosion of softer surrounding rocks and clays, two-hundred-million-year-old logs of stone lie in the Crystal Forest section of Petrified Forest National Park, Arizona.

Right: Detail of a fossilized log in Petrified Forest National Park. Silica in ground water replaced the original tissue in fallen, buried trees, and gradually what was once wood became quartzite, colorfully stained with impurities such as iron and manganese.

*Daybreak at Great Sand Dunes National Monument,
at the base of the Sangre de Cristo Mountains,
Colorado. Some of the dunes here rise seven hundred
feet above adjacent flats.*

*White Sands, New Mexico, suffused with the blue of
dusk. The sun has set behind the San Andres
Mountains in the distance.*

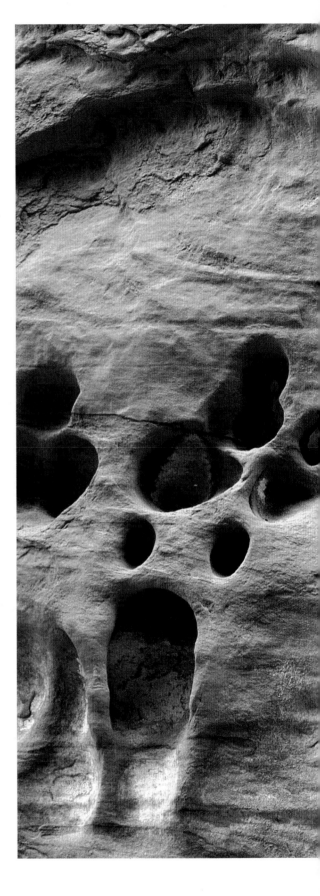

Washed and stained by flash floods, a boulder lies at
the bottom of Paria Canyon. Desert varnish streaks
the sandstone wall in the background.

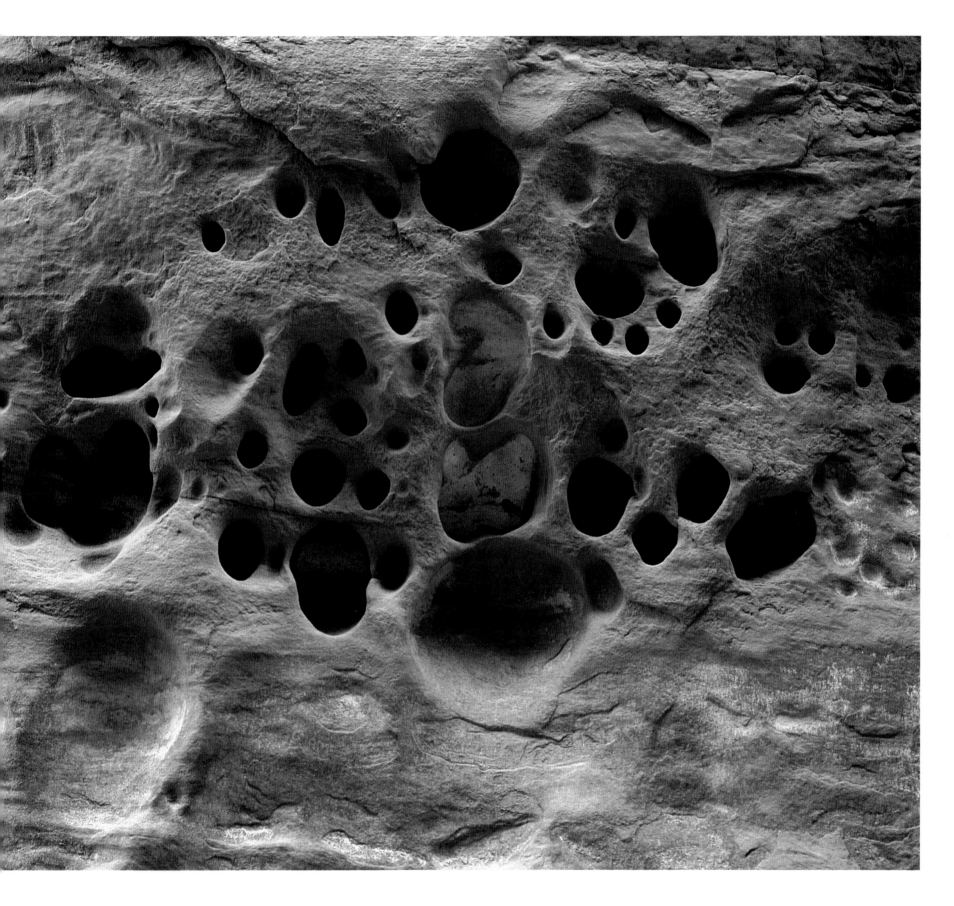

*Eroded sandstone in Paria Canyon, Utah. The
variety of wall details alone makes hiking in most
desert canyons well worth the effort.*

Long Logs area of Petrified Forest National Park,
Arizona. Where now desert exists, massive fossilized
trunks, some more than a hundred feet long, are
evidence of a once-lush forest.

Sunset suffuses the Painted Desert badlands of Chinle mudstone in the northern region of Petrified Forest National Park.

Above: White Sands National Monument contains part of the largest gypsum dune field in the world. Unlike most other sand, the dunes here are firm underfoot, a wonderland for walking.

Right: A cathedral in stone and a potential death trap. This beautiful chamber in a Utah slickrock canyon lies far from any possible escape from the flash floods that occasionally fill it.

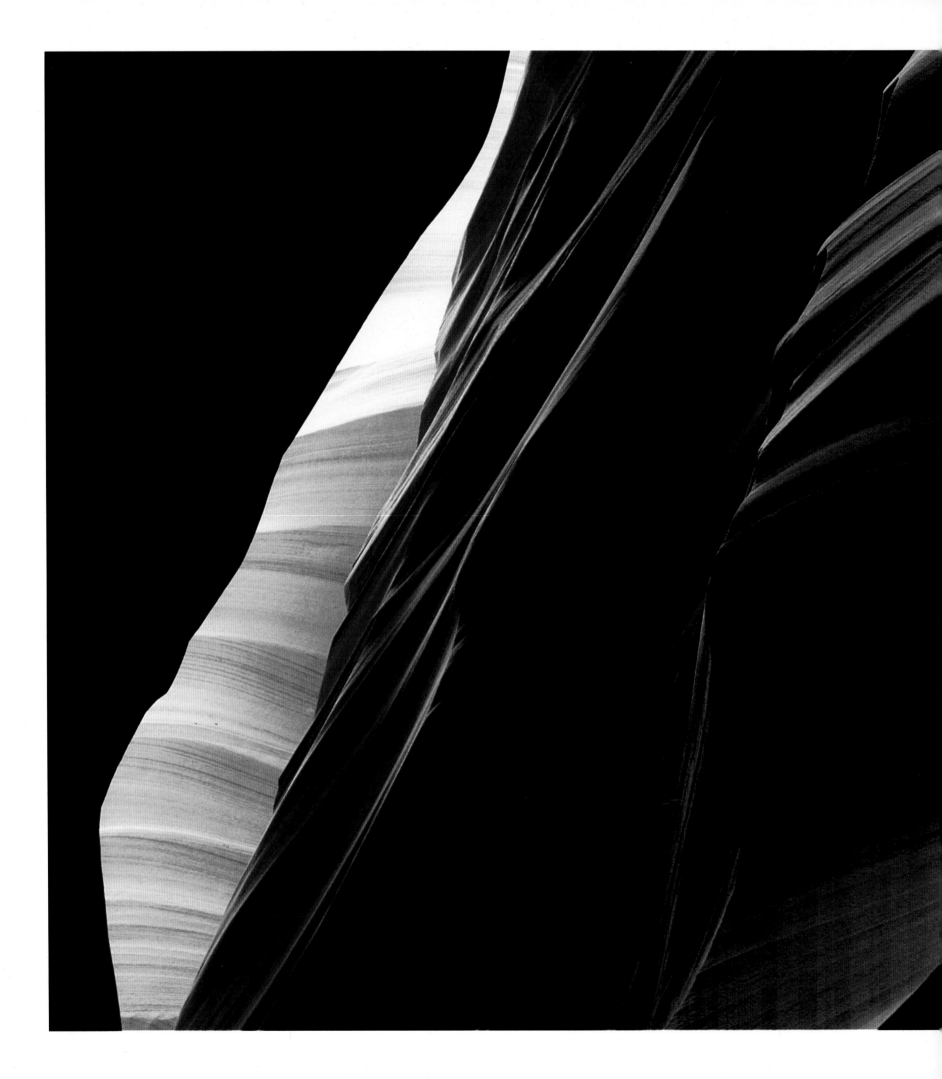

Barely wide enough in places to permit passage sideways, this nameless canyon in northern Arizona is cut into exceptionally fine and delicately striated sandstone.

Inside a flood-carved canyon, delicate textures and
graceful forms evoke those that once must have been
displayed by the desert dunes from which this
sandstone came, many millions of years ago.

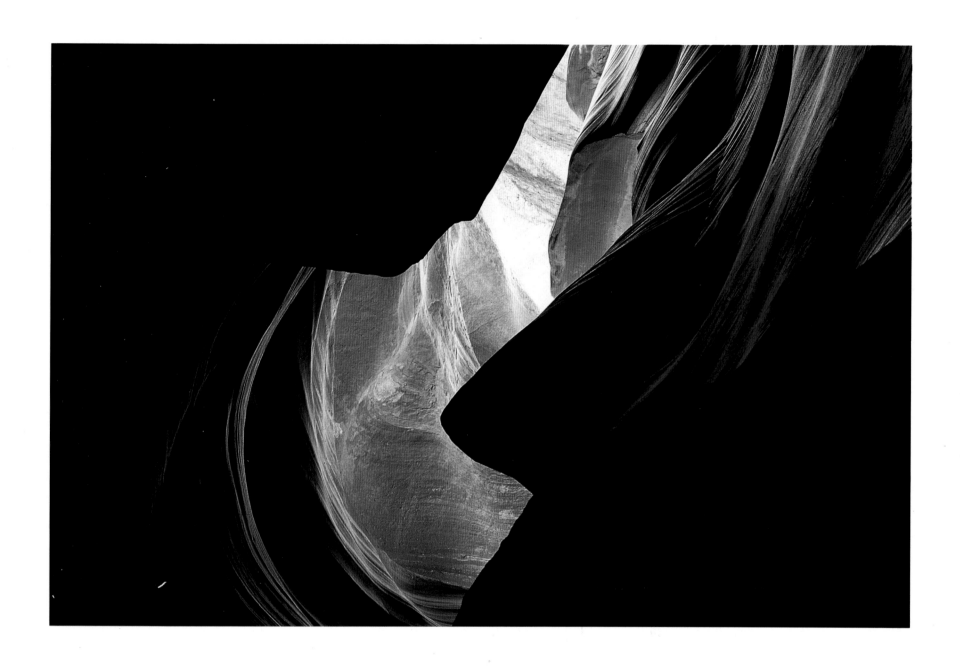

A mix of cool sky light and warm, reflected sunlight creates a blend of rich hues on the walls of another Arizona slot canyon. Well hidden, but easily accessible, this one has suffered the vandalism of bullet holes and graffiti.

In recent decades, water diversions have shrunk
Mono Lake, California, and exposed extensive tufa
formations. The pinnacles were originally formed
under water by the reaction of calcium springs with
carbonates in the lake.

*Dusk at Sunset Crater National Monument,
Arizona. A light snow has dusted this landscape of
delicate volcanic cinders.*

THE LAND OF
SUDDEN SURPRISE

Where the canyon bends, the curving walls lean inwards. A group of hikers has stopped under one such vaulting overhang. It looks like the perfect campsite: a spacious, level platform with views of the surrounding smooth cliffs of orange-tan sandstone. Dust-dry sand gives assurance that the site was completely sheltered from the previous day's light rain. A few easy paces below trickles a clear brook, two or three feet wide and a few inches deep, large by desert standards. Unseen, a massive thunderhead soars just beyond the canyon rim.

The sky falls. Lightning tears through the wet white air as sheets of rain slick the bare, impervious rock. Within two minutes, every groove and trough running off the rounded cliffs spouts a slender waterfall. More than a dozen hundred-foot-high falls are visible to the hikers, including one that takes flight directly over their heads. For the moment, the scene is beautiful and delicate.

Within ten minutes of the arrival of the storm, a much more massive falls crashes to the canyon floor close by. The confluence of scores of instant streams, it is brown and heavy with mud, stones and other debris torn from the land. Meanwhile, runoff has begun to curl under the overhang, drenching the dry sand of the intended tent site. The hikers retreat further into the recess, somewhat concerned now. Upstream, hundreds of cascades must be leaping, tumbling into the canyon.

The brook below has begun to swell, and within twenty minutes it is a raging red-brown river, with standing waves three feet high. Broken branches and the trunks of cottonwood trees bump and bounce in the turbulent, soil-thickened water. Then the storm cloud passes, lightened of its load. The waterfalls disappear with it, except for the large one, which runs another five minutes before stopping abruptly, like a tap shut off. The

Left: The narrowest slot canyons are subterranean corridors aglow with magical, otherworldly light. A climbing rope was used to reach this one, near Page, Arizona.

main stream continues to surge before gradually subsiding over the next hour.

The hikers search for another campsite, selecting the top of a small bench where some mature cottonwoods and a thicket of oaks grow. The site appears safe, not under any potential pour-offs and high enough to have remained undisturbed within recent years. Nonetheless, some of the party privately appraise a nearby sloping cliff buttress, the only accessible retreat from the canyon floor. Sleep comes fitfully, while faint flashes and distant rumblings interrupt the night.

The hikers had been fortunate on two counts. They had seen a spectacular and memorable event, for flash floods are common in the desert but are witnessed by relatively few people. In this case, none of the several other canyons within a few miles' radius had flooded. They were lucky, too, that they had not been caught in a much narrower canyon, one in which a single person, or two people holding hands, can touch both the sheer sides. Walking through such dark conduits, it is not uncommon to pass underneath mud-caked log jams ominously wedged between the walls fifty feet overhead and higher.

A flash flood doesn't necessarily strike where the rain falls. It can funnel in from many miles away and strike under clear skies, out of the blue. Nor does it need a canyon. Where there is scant vegetation and rapid runoff, the shallowest of washes, a slight sag in the land, can be a dangerous place to linger. Flash floods are responsible for the shape of many of the deserts. The landforms are almost all eroded or deposited by water, and water usually comes from the burst of a thunder cell, or not at all.

However, it is in the canyons, most of them dry and without permanent streams, where the flash floods have done their most dramatic work, especially in the slickrock country of the Colorado Plateau. To the wanderer on the desert surface, the canyons can appear without warning, a sudden obstacle that cannot be crossed for many miles. The narrowest, the so-called slot canyons, may appear as little more than black crevasses in the earth, and some, more than a hundred feet deep, can be jumped.

The interiors of these slots are among the most extraordinary places in the desert. The constricted walls block out the sky. Indirect light bounces around the swirled stone chambers, as sound echoes do, creating unexpected effects. The upper reaches of the canyon, where the light is strongest, will be bright yellow. The tone will deepen and the color intensify as the light reflects back and forth between the orange walls, picking up their hue. In the lowest depths, blackness will prevail, with occasional swathes of blue and purple where only the light from the sky directly above, and not the sun, somehow penetrates.

Some of the slot canyons run only a few hundred feet, but look so different with a small change in position or angle of the sun that a passage that takes five minutes to traverse can occupy a photographer for an entire day. Others are sufficiently long to require an overnight excursion. Backpacking through such an endless grand corridor of scalloped sandstone, several hundred feet deep, one can completely lose track of distance and direction, but one cannot get lost. The water channel must continuously descend and eventually exit. A blank wall a couple of hundred feet directly ahead may appear to block the way, and the illusion of an absolute impasse might be maintained until one is but three or four paces away, when a cleft suddenly veers off sharply to one side and the journey continues. One can never be sure what lurks around the next corner. At the least, there could be a sheer drop-off requiring ropes to negotiate, or a very cold pool to swim.

Of the larger canyons, there is a type where an initially meandering stream becomes incised into the rock during a period of geological uplift. Such canyons in sandstone country often contain a sequence of overhangs curving in alternately opposite directions. The grinding floods cut not just downward but also outward as they swing around the bends of the meanders. Each successive flood further undercuts the lengthening canyon wall, resulting in enormous alcoves, half hemispheres with tremendous stone roofs, some of which measure three hundred feet horizontally from the lip to the back of the recess.

Perhaps the surprise canyon explorers most hope to find is that of an ancient Indian ruin or petroglyph. The Anasazi located their dwellings and indeed sometimes entire villages beneath overhanging cliffs. Such impressive sites as Mesa Verde National Park, Canyon de Chelly, Betatakin and Keet Seel are well known, but there are countless smaller ruins, some just a single stone room or a granary hidden in a niche, some still unknown and still undisturbed. All the sites were inexplicably abandoned, and although studies of craft and culture have linked the Anasazi to the Hopi people that live on the mesas of northern Arizona, no one has ever been able to discover why they suddenly left their canyon haunts eight centuries ago.

Cathedral-like spaces exist beneath the desert floor inside slot canyons, such as this one in northern Arizona, for which the evidence on the surface is merely a black crack a few feet across.

Passing through country where the extraordinary lies concealed, this long lonely road eventually leads to the incredible west side of Canyonlands National Park, Utah.

Left: Laden with soil and debris, the runoff from a single storm cloud rages down Davis Gulch, Utah. Before the flash flood, only a tiny trickle flowed in the creek bed.

Above: Willows thrive in a grotto of a tributary canyon of the Escalante River, Utah. Surrounded by deep overhangs, the pool has been excavated by a free-falling waterfall that runs only during flash floods.

Periodic flash floods prevent vegetation from
growing through most of Buckskin Gulch, Utah,
except in elevated niches and wider sections, where
cottonwoods flourish.

A quiet pool along Aztec Creek reflects the high walls near the present-day mouth of Forbidding Canyon, Utah. Like all tributary canyons of Glen Canyon, its once fabulous lower reaches have been lost under the waters of the Lake Powell Reservoir.

49

Left: Moss thrives on the moist, cool wall inside a Utah slot canyon. A couple of hundred feet straight up on the desert surface, it is twenty degrees warmer and cactuses can be found.

Above: Between thunderstorms in Canyonlands National Park, Utah, a rainbow arcs over cliffs streaked with desert varnish.

With over two hundred rooms, Cliff Palace in Mesa
Verde National Park is one of the largest and most
famous of Anasazi ruins. Repaired and reinforced, it
is visited by tens of thousands of visitors every year.

Abandoned probably about eight hundred years ago
and saved by the desert air, its deep sheltering
overhang and its hidden location in a remote,
uninhabited area of southeastern Utah, this
immaculate little Anasazi dwelling is likely known to
only a few dozen people.

The White House Ruin is one of numerous
abandoned Anasazi communities built in deep
recesses at the base of great sandstone walls in
Canyon de Chelly National Monument, Arizona.

Newspaper Rock in San Juan County, Utah, is one of numerous petroglyphs on the Colorado Plateau. Incredibly, many such ancient Indian treasures have been deliberately vandalized.

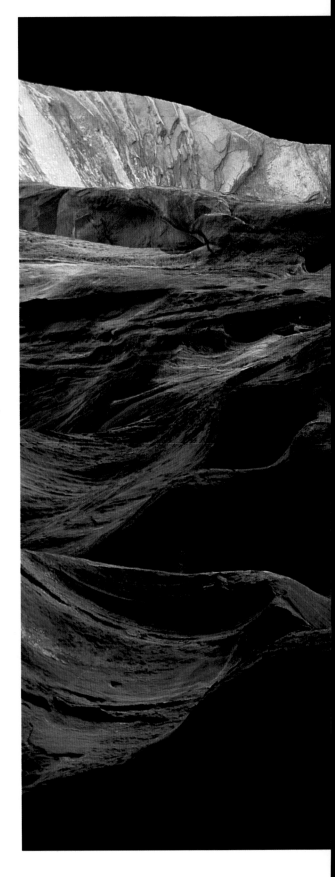

The illusion of a dead-end in Buckskin Gulch, Utah.
The route down the eerie canyon continues beyond
the hiker, occasionally passing under flood-deposited
log jams fifty feet overhead.

A view straight up from the bottom of Buckskin Gulch, where overhanging walls many hundreds of feet high sometimes block out any view of the sky.

Above: The magical interior of an Arizona slot canyon. On the desert surface, it appears as little more than an ominously dark crevasse in the earth.

Right: A small waterfall blocks easy passage up Choal Canyon in northern Arizona.

Above: Buckskin Gulch, Utah, is one of hundreds of sheer-walled canyons carved by desert floods out of the thick sandstone deposits of the Colorado Plateau.

Right: An immense overhang roofs a sharp bend in a canyon in the Escalante Wilderness, Utah. At the far end of the grotto, Lobo Arch spans 175 feet.

The convoluted, incised slickrock wilderness east of the Escalante River in Utah. Even viewed from the air, much of the landscape remains hidden in deep canyons and roofed alcoves.

The Goosenecks area of the San Juan River, seen from the air. In many parts of the Colorado Plateau, uplift of flat country rejuvenated old, lazy streams and caused their meanders to cut deeply into the land.

63

Left: Kaibito Creek cuts grooves in the solid
sandstone floor of its canyon near Page, Arizona.

Above: The colors of warm sandstone walls and
green cottonwoods and horsetails are reflected in the
waters of Kaibito Creek, a large stream by desert
canyon standards.

HIDDEN RIVER,
LOST RIVER

The route heads due north across an ordinary plain studded with sage and juniper. The land rises slightly and passes through a forest of ponderosa pine. A few miles farther on, the traveler comes to Mather Point. Apart from a safety railing and a parking lot, there is not much to indicate that there is anything remarkable to see.

Perhaps the traveler has visited the Himalayas, the plains of East Africa, the Land of the Midnight Sun. But nothing, absolutely nothing the traveler could ever have experienced can prepare him for those few steps up to the railing. Suddenly the earth rushes away, and he confronts an abrupt immensity, a hundred great cliffs in one gaze, an apparently endless series of fall-offs dropping out of the bright afternoon down through corridors of blue shadow and into dark abysses far below. If the world were flat and had an edge, it might look like this. If there were a single place on earth where the day began and the day ended, it would be here.

Sunrise, sunset at the rim of the Grand Canyon—at dawn and at dusk, the spacious viewpoints can be unexpectedly crowded. The canyon is a mood, more powerful than place. Much more than spectacle, it stirs the spirit.

There are many canyons deeper than the Grand Canyon, and some that are wider or longer, but the Grand Canyon is beyond statistics and unique. Perhaps it can be said to be the greatest surprise on earth. The sudden arrival at the brink has shocked travelers since 1540, when Coronado's Spaniards, intent on plunder, had the Europeans' first encounter with the chasm. One of the paradoxes of the Grand Canyon is that, while immense enough to contain mountains, fifty yards back from the rim it may betray no hint of its existence.

Left: Late December, Monument Canyon near the bottom of the Grand Canyon, Arizona. The climate here is mild; the snow-dusted cliffs in the background are evidence of a cold winter on the rim high above.

The Grand Canyon is, in fact, not one canyon, but hundreds. Every mile or so along the 278-mile length of the main gorge, a tributary canyon joins in. The larger of these side canyons in turn branch off into their own side canyons, the net result being a labyrinth of buttes, buttresses and breaches out of which it is sometimes impossible to distinguish the main channel of the Colorado River. And along the section where the canyon is widest, some 18 miles across, the Colorado River is the least apparent from the rim, indeed entirely invisible from some viewpoints. The river that has made one of the greatest cuts on the earth's surface is a hidden river.

Perhaps the best way to appreciate the size and the range of the Grand Canyon is to descend one of the trails down to the river, down to another climate, another world. The temperature difference between top and bottom is the same as that between Canada and Mexico; and in a typical winter, the higher North Rim might get a dozen feet of snow, the South Rim half of that, while the Colorado River in between, but a full mile below, gets none.

A hike into the canyon is a walk across latitudes, but also a walk through geological time. The descent takes one from the pale Kaibab limestone, through the Toroweap formation and ocher Coconino sandstone, across purple Hermit shale, down through the Orange Supai group and past stupendous cliffs of Redwall limestone, down steps of yellow Muav limestone, out onto the greenish Bright Angel shale of the Tonto Platform and over a lip of brown Tapeats sandstone for the final drop into the inner Gorge at the bottom of which lies dense, dark, durable Vishnu schist, rock 1,700 million years old. Each stride on the day-long descent spans, on average, 100,000 years of the earth's history.

On the banks of the Colorado, which seems deceptively small in front of massive cliffs, one might muse on how long it took the river to saw its way through stone to reach this depth. In the answer lies perhaps the most surprising paradox of the Grand Canyon. For while the canyon is often thought of as being very ancient, indeed almost eternal, it is, in contrast to the rock it exposes, very young. By some estimates, it has taken the Colorado a mere four million years to carve the canyon, a nearly insignificant amount of time in comparison to the age of the earth, or indeed of other features on the planet, such as most mountain ranges. Dinosaur bones, for instance, are dozens of times older than the canyon.

The erosive power of the Colorado is evident in its wild, lunging rapids. Once it was very evident in the dense brown of its silt-laden waters, waters that in some years carried as much as a million tons of sediment a day past gauging stations. But the quality of the water is not what it used to be. A sieve has been installed in the river, and the natural balance of erosion and deposition has been altered. There is a dam in the desert.

Glen Canyon Dam blocks the Colorado upstream from the Grand Canyon and continues, a quarter century after its completion, to provoke one of the most bitter environmental debates in history. For the Grand Canyon was not the only canyon that the Colorado created. It passed through Westwater, Cataract, Narrow and Glen canyons before entering Marble Canyon, the upstream portion of Grand Canyon.

Dead Horse Point near Moab, Utah, above Cataract Canyon, looks out over a sweeping bend in the Colorado River. The broken, stepped, red and yellow cliffs interrupted here and there by shrub-speckled benches are surprisingly reminiscent of the Grand Canyon, which begins more than two hundred miles downstream. But the scenery is not similar all along the course of the Colorado. In between lies a region dominated by monolithic sandstone, and a landscape that looks more sculptured than eroded.

This is where Glen Canyon used to be. In its other canyons, only experienced whitewater adventurers dare navigate the roller-coaster rapids, but the Colorado River flowed quietly here. Accessible to all who loved the desert, it slid past sandy beaches and cottonwood groves and under smooth monumental walls. Twisting side canyons led to great chambers, in shadow yet suffused with the warm glow of light reflected off orange sandstone. Enclosed by massive, curving overhangs, sometimes containing a reflecting pool, a delicate waterfall at the upstream end, or a moss and fern-adorned seep, these were achingly beautiful places, places with names like Music Temple and Cathedral in the Desert.

Many of those who were born in time to see it claim for Glen Canyon and its tributaries a more singular beauty than even the Grand Canyon itself. Arguably, it contained the finest desert landscapes in the United States. Today, the Lake Powell Reservoir replaces Glen Canyon. The waters behind the dam have also inundated several hundred side canyons, the relatively short Narrow Canyon and the lower reaches of Cataract Canyon on the Colorado, as well as much of the canyon of the San Juan River, a major tributary.

There won't always be a reservoir here. Studies of the tremendous sediment loads of the Colorado drainage basin predict that Lake Powell will be filled in with silt within a couple of centuries. Proponents of Glen Canyon Dam believe it was worthwhile for the access to previously remote areas the reservoir supposedly provides, for a few generations at least. But these places compare poorly to those that now lie under the water where the power boats whine. The best of the desert and the best of the river have been lost forever.

Cliffs and buttes hide the Colorado River in scenery reminiscent of the Grand Canyon, south of Arches National Park, Utah.

Toroweap Overlook at dawn. The Colorado River here lies three thousand feet below the stupendous cliff.

Above: A pair of junipers, one dead, the other living, along the South Rim of the Grand Canyon. Cold December mist diffuses the sunrise.

Right: A redbud tree blooms along Boulder Creek, far down in the Grand Canyon. The species flowers for only one week in the spring.

Pink-blossomed redbuds and fresh-leaved cottonwoods thrive near the springs of Indian Gardens below the South Rim.

The mid-morning sun illuminates cottonwoods along
Bright Angel Creek near Phantom Ranch at the
bottom of the Grand Canyon.

Pouring over travertine terraces at its base, Havasu Falls is one of several exquisite cascades in Havasu Canyon, one of the largest side canyons of the Grand Canyon.

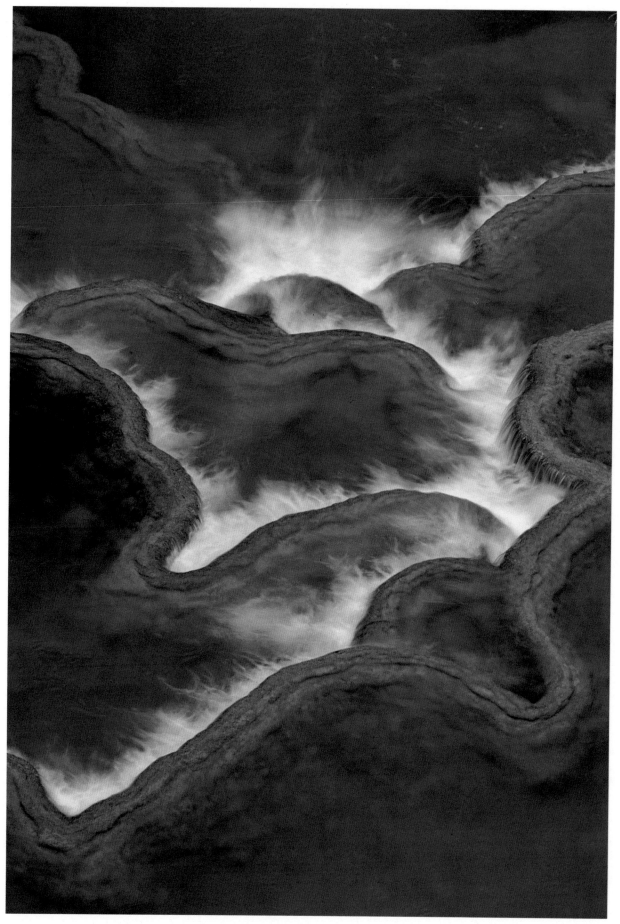

The travertine terraces at the base of Havasu Falls, seen from the top.

An aerial view of Zoroaster Temple (nearest), Brahma Temple and Deva Temple, with the cliffs below the Walhalla Plateau in the far distance.

Above: Brahma Temple, Zoroaster Temple and the South Rim from Bright Angel Point, some time after sunset.

Right: Angels' Gate from the air, with the North Rim at the top of the picture. This great chasm is merely a side canyon of Clear Creek, which in turn is one of a great number of canyons of the Grand Canyon.

Above: Morning sunlight breaks through an overcast sky to illuminate Cope Butte and other parts of the Grand Canyon, viewed from an overlook along the Great Mojave Wall.

Right: A downstream view from Toroweap Overlook. In this portion of the Grand Canyon, lava flows from the right occasionally dammed the Colorado River in prehistoric times.

The view from Point Imperial early in the morning. The prominent butte in the near distance is Mount Hayden.

Zoroaster Temple and Brahma Temple, two of the
most recognizable landmarks within the Grand
Canyon, seen here from a small airplane against the
diffused light of the setting sun.

Set against the deep shadow of Wotan's Throne, a buttress below Cape Royal catches the light of the rising sun. The south side of the Grand Canyon is in the far distance.

Cliffs of the South Rim, the upper layers vivid in the morning sun, soar above the Bright Angel Trail.

A tiny part of the vast landscape of cliffs and plateaus of the Grand Canyon, taken from Toroweap looking south across the chasm.

*Desert View, near the east entrance to Grand Canyon
National Park, offers a sweeping panorama across
one of the wider sections of the canyon, where it
bends from a southerly to a westerly direction.*

MOUNTAINS AND MONUMENTS

While much of the desert is level, there is grandeur below its plateaus, in the caverns and the canyons, in the descending places where the land seems to step downward forever. And there is as much grandeur again above the desert, where stone climbs into the sky, to sit in defiance of probability on the tops of monuments and on the summits of mountains.

There is no scarcity of mountains in the southwest. Indeed, despite extensive flats and plateau areas, it is hard to find a place in the open desert from which a mountain cannot be seen, if only in the far distance.

The geography of Nevada in particular is a repeating sequence of basin and range, basin and range. Here, the crust of the earth is slowly being stretched by complex continental movements, to the point where it is one of the thinnest areas on the planet. The resulting stress has created alternating peaks and troughs across the Great Basin from California to Utah, a vast, sparsely populated region with no outlet to the sea.

For the traveler, the Great Basin might at first seem monotonous. Every crest and trough seems to resemble the last, and roads can be seen to run dead straight across the treeless basins for fifteen miles without the slightest curve or jog. But the land soon becomes awesome in a disconcerting way. Gas stations are farther apart than on roads in Alaska, and it is quite possible, in the middle of the day on a major, paved highway, to drive for half an hour without encountering another vehicle or passing a single dwelling; in fact, to be the only person in an area of more than a thousand square miles. Here is an impressive wilderness, but one demanding too much fortitude and offering too little surprise to be worth wandering on foot.

The mountains of the Great Basin and of the other desert regions share characteristics different from those common to most of the other ranges of the continent. There are no lush blankets of forest leading up to the lake-

Left: Vishnu Temple, one of many great buttes in the Grand Canyon as large as mountains, seen from the air at sunset.

dappled depressions and the hanging valleys of a glacial landscape. Instead rapid runoff has cut densely branching networks of gullies and ridges out of the spare slopes, like pleated skirts that have been heavily wrinkled. With no permanent rivers to carry the washed-down debris away, desert ranges rise out of bajadas, gradual and very evenly spread slopes of overlapping alluvial fans that encircle the mountains.

The intricate erosion patterns of the upper slopes and the miles-long slopes of the bajadas fool the eye, and the mountains of the desert are, for the most part, much bigger than they appear. Telescope Peak is perhaps the best example. At 11,049 feet, it towers more than two vertical miles, or twice the depth of the Grand Canyon, above the salt flats of Death Valley, 282 feet below sea level. This is the greatest base-to-summit elevation difference of any mountain in the lower forty-eight states, and about the same as that between Base Camp and the summit of Mount Everest. Yet in the clear desert air, without the asset of steep cleavage or dazzling glaciers, Telescope Peak is less striking than many others that are lesser in size.

Among the latter would be included some relatively small peaks such as the Ajo Range in Organ Pipe Cactus National Monument, the Superstition Mountains near Phoenix and the Chisos Mountains in Big Bend National Park. Monumental chisels and teeth, these sharp peaks are noteworthy for their cragginess. Others, well-known landmarks such as Baboquivari Peak west of Tucson and El Capitan in Guadalupe National Park, are impressive for their big cliff faces.

Among the greatest cliffs in the desert are those of Zion National Park. Zion is a canyon, but its very high walls are eroded into separate features, such as the sheer Mount Kinesava, West Temple, Towers of the Virgin, Three Patriarchs and the Great White Throne.

Of all the mountains associated with the desert, none are grander than those of the Sierra Nevada. In their rain shadow, the Mojave and Great Basin deserts begin. The dry side of this magnificent granite range, the east escarpment, rises nearly two miles above the desert and runs for more than a hundred miles parallel to Owens Valley and beyond. Outside Alaska, it is the greatest mountain barrier in the United States and has the highest summit, Mount Whitney at 14,495 feet.

But grandeur does not depend on scale, on immensity. It can result from shape as much as from size. On the opposite, eastern side of the Great Basin Desert from the Sierra Nevada is a rock, a piece of Entrada sandstone no taller than a small apartment building, which inspires as much awe and silent reverence as the deepest canyon or the tallest mountain. Delicate Arch in Arches National Park is the ultimate example of balancing stone. Gracefully, it vaults high and clear along a narrow ridge where a sheer cliff drops off on one side and a steep-sided bowl lies on the other. Thus poised between brinks, it is completely without buttresses of any kind, connected to the earth only at two small bases. A triumph of the inanimate against the inflexible laws of gravity and of chance, it seems suspended in both space and time.

There are more than sixty stone arches in Arches National Park, including Landscape Arch, a remarkably thin and nearly horizontal slab spanning the length of a football field. Either Landscape Arch or Kolob Arch in Zion frames the widest rock opening in the world, depending on the measurement criteria accepted. Altogether, southern Utah and northern Arizona have nine arches or natural bridges straddling more than two hundred feet. Of the second, Natural Bridges National Monument alone has three: Sipapu, Kachina and Owachomo, while famous Rainbow Bridge is the most massive natural span in the world and the longest across a watercourse.

There are many arches and natural bridges on the Colorado Plateau, including several magnificent ones in Canyonlands National Park. Here are also great numbers of rock spires and standing slabs, at times suggesting hundreds of huge chessmen or a petrified city. Along with some elaborately convoluted canyons and the junction of the looping Colorado and Green rivers, the landscape of Canyonlands is too complex to be readily described.

Rock standing upright occurs on a very impressive scale in the skyscrapers of de Chelly sandstone in Monument Valley. An abundance of thousand-foot high buttes and towers and one remarkable thin, tall pillar constitute the sheer-sided, eroded remnants of what was once an uplifted and fractured plateau. To the south of Monument Valley stand a few other rock towers of quite different manufacture. Black and craggy, they are volcanic necks, the cores of ancient volcanoes. Agathla Needle is the largest of these, surpassed only by famous Shiprock, some seventy miles to the east in New Mexico.

Its abundance of extraordinary rock formations and canyons gives the Colorado Plateau a grandeur as awesome as that of the greatest of mountain ranges or the wildest of seas. Out of that richness it would be quite arbitrary to single out one place. However, one that is the favorite of many people is Bryce Canyon National Park. A fantasy land of rock minarets and castles, it is succinctly described by the Indian name for the place: "red rocks like standing men in a bowl-shaped amphitheater," although the color of the landscape is a subtle blend of oranges, yellows, pinks and lavenders. Across the up-and-down rhythm of slender and joined rock staffs, one can distinguish the horizontal lines of a lake-deposited geology. One visitor perhaps described the place best. "It looks like music," she said.

Rainbow Bridge in southern Utah is one of the greatest natural rock arches on earth, spanning nearly three hundred feet.

Right: Sunrise from Inspiration Point. The numerous overlooks in Bryce Canyon National Park, Utah, are especially spectacular in the morning.

Part of the eastern escarpment of the Sierra Nevada, silhouetted at dusk near Big Pine, California. The Mojave and Great Basin deserts begin in the rain shadow of this high range.

The morning sun pokes through one of the gaps in Druid Arch, Canyonlands National Park, Utah. The spectacular formation consists of vertical slabs of rock several hundred feet high.

*The Rainbow Plateau on the Utah-Arizona
boundary is one of the most formidably rugged parts
of the Colorado Plateau, with deep, convoluted
canyons cutting through a region dense with steep-
sided slickrock domes.*

A thunderhead explodes skyward over the eastern Sierra Nevada, California.

Left: Seen from the air, cloud shadows and afternoon light enhance the already dramatic landscape of Monument Valley, Arizona, where sheer-sided monoliths stand a thousand feet high.

Above: Seen from overhead, Yei-Bichei and Totem Pole cast shadows across the floor of Monument Valley. The slender rock pillars are several hundred feet high.

Above: Snow lingers in May in the shaded gullies of Bryce Canyon, where a number of deeply eroded bowls have been carved from the Pink Cliffs.

Right: One of innumerable standing pillars of stone in Bryce Canyon National Park, Utah, during an April snowfall.

Like immense chessmen, towers of rock about four
hundred feet high stand in the prairie of Chesler
Park. These are but a few of hundreds of such
formations in the Needles district of Canyonlands
National Park.

One of the most convoluted and bewilderingly
dissected landscapes anywhere, the Maze district of
Canyonlands National Park, Utah, can perhaps only
be fully comprehended from the air.

Partition Arch is one of more than eighty natural arches in Arches National Park.

Red Arch Mountain, part of the vertical world of Navajo sandstone in Zion National Park, Utah.

Very soft sandstone in Cathedral Gorge State Park,
Nevada, has been severely eroded into crumbling but
spectacular formations.

Pre-eminent among the many cliffs in Zion National Park is the Great White Throne, rising a sheer half mile above its base.

An overhead view of the hoodoo land of Bryce Canyon National Park, showing how erosion has carved up the escarpment of the Pink Cliffs.

A tiny fraction of the forest of hoodoos that fill Bryce Amphitheater in Bryce Canyon National Park.

Near Kayenta, Arizona, stand the eroded cores of ancient volcanoes that periodically erupted as the North American continental plate moved over a stationary hot spot deep within the earth. The most distant one on the right is Agathla Needle, the highest in this group.

The eastern escarpment of the Sierra Nevada from Lone Pine, California. This great mountain range towers as much as two miles in altitude above Owens Valley.

*The setting sun fires the cliffs of the Watchman at the
south entrance to Zion National Park, Utah.*

114

Arches National Park, Utah, contains many impressive standing rock features. Balanced Rock, on the right, has been estimated to weigh more than 3,500 tons.

DESERT MOON, DESERT BLOOM

The organ pipe cactus loves the sun, the intense light, the heat, the dryness. It grows best on wide-open south-facing slopes in a baked land, ranging no farther north than southernmost Arizona. But its large, delicate flowers open only after sunset, after a rain. So too the saguaro, the stately symbol of Arizona, and the night-blooming cereus, which flowers only during a single night in June.

With darkness comes coolness. Gone is the shriveling heat: the air temperatures that in some regions exceed 120° F, while surface temperatures may reach 200° F, forcing insects to remain airborne and everything else that is mobile to hide.

Dusk breaks the searing silence of the day. Trills and beeps from toads issue out of moist pockets. The haunting hoot of an owl echoes and re-echoes off slickrock canyon walls. A correspondence of coyote howls rises suddenly to an eerily beautiful chorus coming from ambiguous directions. In the light of the moon, the foragers and the hunters pursue their assignments, prey and predator alike captive to the ageless, unbreakable cycles that outlast all species.

The wildlife of the desert is surprisingly diverse. There are mice, gophers, jack rabbits, badgers, javelinas, coatis, deer, bighorn sheep, bobcats and cougars. There used to be jaguars. They are now extinct north of the Mexican border and rare south of it. Many of the prominent animals, however, while found in the desert, are not of the desert, but merely capable of adapting to it. They range elsewhere, particularly the mammals and birds. The most famous exception among the mammals is the kangaroo rat, always noted for the fact that it doesn't need to drink in its entire lifetime because it has the amazing capability to metabolize water out of the food it eats.

Particularly identified with the desert are certain reptiles and arachnids: rattlesnakes and lizards, scorpions and tarantulas. But ultimately, it is not by their creatures that deserts are distinguished. Although the night is alive with the activity of fauna, it is the photosynthesis of flora by day

Left: A standing snag in the Patriarch Grove of the Bristlecone Pine Forest, White Mountains, California.

that defines the deserts. The limits of the Sonoran, Mojave, Great Basin and Chihuahuan deserts are reckoned chiefly on the basis of the plants that grow there.

And a great variety of plants there are, despite the fact that deserts are, by definition, areas of sparse vegetation. The Sonoran Desert alone has 2,500 different species. Among these are many cactuses, including the organ pipe and the famous saguaro. The former, abundant in Mexico, is found only in and around Organ Pipe Cactus National Monument north of the border in Arizona. In that state, it is upstaged even in its own preserve by the more common and taller saguaro, which can reach a height of fifty feet, weigh many tons and live more than two hundred years. Known for its classic branching form, which generally doesn't begin to develop until after a century of growth, the saguaro can occasionally develop as many as four dozen arms.

Perhaps the most surprising fact about the saguaro is that, while it grows out in the open, it is never fully exposed to the desert sun. The rows of dense spines, which serve a secondary role in helping protect the cactus from being eaten, have their most important function in shielding the fleshy green body from solar rays and desiccating winds. Casting tiny shadows by the thousands, the spines ensure that, to a large degree, the saguaro grows in the shade.

The desert is home to some of the most exotic of plants. Along with many kinds of cactus, there are other succulents such as the agaves, including the century plant, which grows for many years as a succulent at ground level before sending up a towering stalk of blossoms and then dying. Various kinds of yuccas are prominent, including the Joshua tree. The graceful stalks of ocotillo are common in some regions.

But the most common plants in the desert are bushes of various kinds: saltbush, rabbitbrush, sagebrush, blackbush, mesquite. The creosote bush is the prevalent plant of the Sonoran Desert, perfectly adapted to the arid land with extensive root systems and the ability to die back during long dry periods and resurface when more moisture is available.

Perhaps stranger to contemplate than the plants of the desert themselves are the contrasting environments found within a short distance in the desert. The mountain environment is well known for the proximity of different biomes, resulting from great changes in altitude. The desert has its share of mountains, but in a curious way: the usual pattern of forests' giving way to treeless terrain is here reversed. The desert mountains, being cooler and catching more precipitation at higher altitudes, are the refuges of forests. Here, one comes to the timberline and enters the woods in ascending a mountain, rather than the other way around.

Much more marked than in the mountains, however, are the life transitions in the canyons. Whereas in the former, a mile gain in altitude will result in a drop of about 20° F, the same difference can be found a couple of hundred feet apart between the rim of a canyon and its cool, inner recesses. Here, moss, ferns and horsetail may grow in the shadows immediately below cactuses in the sun. Along the wet canyon bottoms are often found lush groves of cottonwoods, the oases of the American deserts.

In spite of its harshness and the fact that by definition the desert is a wasteland, the desert allows for a tremendous variety of life. There is life that ventures forth in the moonlight and life that could only survive in the shadows, but of it all, the most magnificent is the life that bursts forth after a rain. It is the rain that permits life to continue in the desert, the rain that brings the bloom. In the spring, in late summer, until November and as early as February, rain can bring forth flowers. There are the lavish, showy blossoms of the cactuses and the smaller but more numerous flowers of poppies, lilies, owlclover, goldfields and many more that carpet the ground in swells of vivid color. Some of the greatest floral displays occur in places that, most of the time, are the driest and most desolate, like the Sonoran Desert around the lower reaches of the Colorado.

A bloom can erupt profusely when triggered by the rain at the right time, but it is a rare and short-lived celebration. A truly spectacular bloom may happen only once or twice in a decade.

Of all the plants, of all the living things in the desertlands of America, perhaps the most venerable is one that is not technically a desert plant. Never growing below 7,500 feet and reaching altitudes of 12,000 feet, the bristlecone pine is a subalpine species. But it attains its finest form in the mountains of the desert, particularly the White Mountains in eastern California and ranges in Nevada. In the meeting of two severe, spare environments, that of the high mountains and that of desert, it grows very slowly. But on bare rocky slopes, in the clean, dry, thin air, it knows neither fire nor disease nor rot. And it needs only a thin strip of bark on an otherwise naked, wind blasted trunk to connect it to the life-sustaining ground and keep it growing indefinitely. Gnarled, twisted sculptures of hard wood swirled in gold, gray and rust, the weather-beaten snags and living specimens are more landscape than tree; as enduring as rock, as inviting of contemplation as sandstone canyon walls.

Thus the bristlecone pines survive as the oldest living things on earth. Some bristlecones are more than 4,000 years old, and at least one (which was cut down by a researcher) is known to have exceeded 5,000 years in age. Such trees were already very, very old at the time of Christ or Buddha. The parent trees of some bristlecone pines were already thriving at the end of the last Ice Age. In the desert mountains grow trees that have lived as long as a thousand desert blooms, as long as fifty thousand desert moons.

Left: *An elevated niche allows spring green trees to grow in an otherwise narrow, flood-scoured slot canyon in southern Utah.*

Above: *Nama blossoms amidst a talus slope of sandstone boulders in an Arizona canyon. The plant is an annual, going from seed to seed in a single year, and may not appear if there is insufficient rain.*

Claret cup cactus, Arizona. A very spiny plant, its blossoms are nearly identical to those of a relative with very few spines.

Aspens near Betatakin Ruin in Navajo National Monument, Arizona. In the deep, cold shade of Segi Canyon, these trees have yet to leaf out, while spring has arrived on the rim above.

A bristlecone pine at dawn on an exposed ridge at 11,000 feet in the White Mountains of California. While most of the tree is dead, it will probably continue to thrive for many centuries.

Gnarled, weather-beaten specimens of bristlecone pine are extraordinarily photogenic; each one can be contemplated for hours from countless angles. This is the same tree pictured on the opposite page.

Above: Desert paintbrush blossoms from a crack in Entrada sandstone in Arches National Park, Utah.

Right: A Parry's agave, or century plant, below the Chisos Mountains in Big Bend National Park, Texas. After growing for many years, the hefty succulent will blossom by growing a spectacular flower stalk a dozen feet high.

Left: A thunderstorm brews over Canyonlands National Park, Utah, in October. This late in the year, this far north, the desert floor can be colorful with flowers.

Above: Cholla cactus and ocotillo in Tucson Mountain Park, Arizona. The fresh green leaves of the ocotillo indicate a recent rainfall.

*Amidst the red rocks of Valley of Fire State Park,
Nevada, plant life is spare and widely scattered.*

*A grove of cottonwoods flourishes in the canyon of
Calf Creek near Boulder, Utah, while widely
scattered junipers dot the slickrock expanses above.*

Plant communities thrive in troughs between dunes
at White Sands National Monument. Prominent here
are specimens of the soaptree yucca, state flower of
New Mexico.

A fresh snowfall clings to the delicate branches of trees in Refrigerator Canyon, Zion National Park.

Left: A saguaro cactus in Saguaro National Monument, Arizona. Stately specimens can sometimes reach heights of fifty feet and live several hundred years.

Above: While the oldest living bristlecone pine ever recorded exceeded five thousand years in age, fallen snags may contain wood twice as old. Tree-ring analysis of these trees has thus provided climate records a hundred centuries into the past.

Cottonwoods flourish in the wide alcoves of Coyote Gulch near Escalante, Utah.

North of Escalante, Utah. Cottonwoods bring
autumn color to a landscape already richly colored in
geology.

Siphoned off to Los Angeles, the receding waters of Mono Lake have left behind towers of tufa and a moist shoreline lush with attractive grasses but have created a very serious ecological crisis for wildlife.

Resembling yuccas except for the finer blossoms on their flower stalks, bear grasses, or nolinas, abound in the rocky landscape near the Santa Maria Canyon, Arizona.

Above: Fresh blossoms of evening primrose in West Canyon, Arizona. The delicate white petals will quickly shrivel and become pink.

Right: Sacred datura, or jimsonweed, grows in a muddy depression in the Valley of Fire, Nevada. The species can bloom any time from May to November.

Above: Saguaro, organ pipe and cholla cactuses grow on the bajadas below the Ajo Range in Organ Pipe Cactus National Monument, Arizona.

Right: The flowers of widely scattered desert buckwheat are matched in vividness by the Vermilion Cliffs in the Painted Desert, Arizona.

Dense rows of spines backlit by the late afternoon sun create golden glows around saguaro and cholla cactuses in Organ Pipe National Monument.